The Whisper of the Stars

Written by Janine Scott
Photography by Bryan and Cherry Alexander

Russia

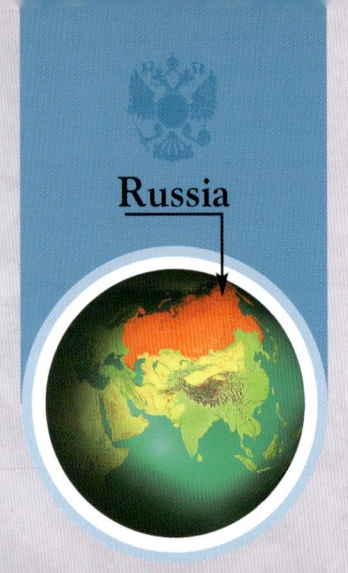

Lena comes from Siberia in Russia. Many Siberian children are used to living with snow and ice for much of the year. Lena's town is one of the coldest towns on Earth. At certain times of the year, it gets so cold that it can be dangerous even to play outside. Lena's friendships help her endure these hard times.

friendship making and keeping friends

Contents

The Whisper of the Stars   4

Explore Russia   14

Beautiful Buildings   16

The Ballet   18

The Royals of Russia   20

Russia on the Move   22

What Do You Think?   24

Index   24

The Whisper of the Stars

My name is Lena. I live in Siberia. My town is called Verkhoyansk (Verk ho YANSK). It is one of the coldest towns in the world. It can get so cold that your breath freezes instantly!

The symbol for our town is bull horns, which relates to an old Siberian legend. In this legend, winter looks like a big bull made of ice and snow. The bull has large horns and cold breath.

Verkhoyansk made history in 1885. It experienced the coldest weather ever recorded. It was -90.4°F!

Did You Know?

If boiling water is thrown into the air when temperatures are -63°F or below, the water turns to ice immediately.

When temperatures are -63°F or below, the cold, dry air causes the vapor in breath to turn to ice crystals. The resulting noise sounds like grain being poured. The local people call this sound the Whisper of the Stars.

My family and I are Yakuts. We are one of the indigenous peoples of Siberia. To keep warm and dry, we wear coats, mittens, scarfs, fur hats, and boots made from reindeer skin. Sometimes we wear so many clothes that only our eyes can be seen!

Our family name is Potapov, and my last name is Potapova. This is because Russian girls and women add the letter "a" to their last names.

indigenous   belonging to a particular place

Even one of the coldest towns on Earth has a school. The school is close to my home. My favorite subject is English. I also learn Russian and my native language. When it is very, very cold, the youngest children do not have to go to school. If temperatures drop below -76°F, our school closes, and we all stay at home!

Does your school ever close in bad weather?

Everyone in our family has chores to do. My dad milks our cows, pours the milk into bowls, and leaves the bowls outside. Then my sister and I bring the frozen milk inside.

Our five cows live in a heated shed. Things freeze so quickly where I live that we give the cows hot water to drink!

Supplies for our town's stores come in by road and river. Helicopters also deliver supplies, but they can't fly when temperatures are below -43°F. My sister and I love buying our bread because the ovens keep the bakery warm.

Our water comes in frozen blocks. Some people buy their frozen river water, but my family gets our own river ice. We break it into chunks and carry it home on our sled. Then we melt the ice into drinking water. It is very clean water, so we do not need to boil it.

Suited to the Cold

Yakut horses live in the Arctic. Their short, stocky bodies and thick hair help them live in the bitter cold. Tame Yakut horses are groomed. However, it is usually to remove ice from their coats, rather than dirt.

Reindeer eat moss, which contains a chemical that keeps their body fluids from freezing.

Yakut horses and reindeer survive the Siberian winters. What other animals are adapted to live in the cold? What traits help them?

Despite the cold outside, we can walk around in our T-shirts inside. Our house is warmed by both a furnace and a wood fire. We do not need a freezer in our house. During winter, we store our food outside. In summer, our food is kept in a cellar that is dug under the permafrost in the ground.

permafrost   a layer of soil under the surface that stays frozen all year round

What would you miss if you had to spend so much time indoors?

In very cold weather, the children in our town have to stay inside, because their lungs can freeze! My two sisters and I read, listen to music, play games, and watch television. We also play with our pets. Since we are inside so much, we have learned to be good friends and to get along well. We look forward to the short summer, when we can play outside with our friends.

Explore Russia

Russia is the biggest country in the world by area. It stretches 6,000 miles, from Europe in the west to the Pacific Ocean in the east.

Russia has many different climates. In some parts of Russia, the winters are extremely long and cold. These parts are covered with snow and ice for more than half the year. The summers in these parts can be warm, but they are short. In other parts of Russia, the weather can be extremely hot.

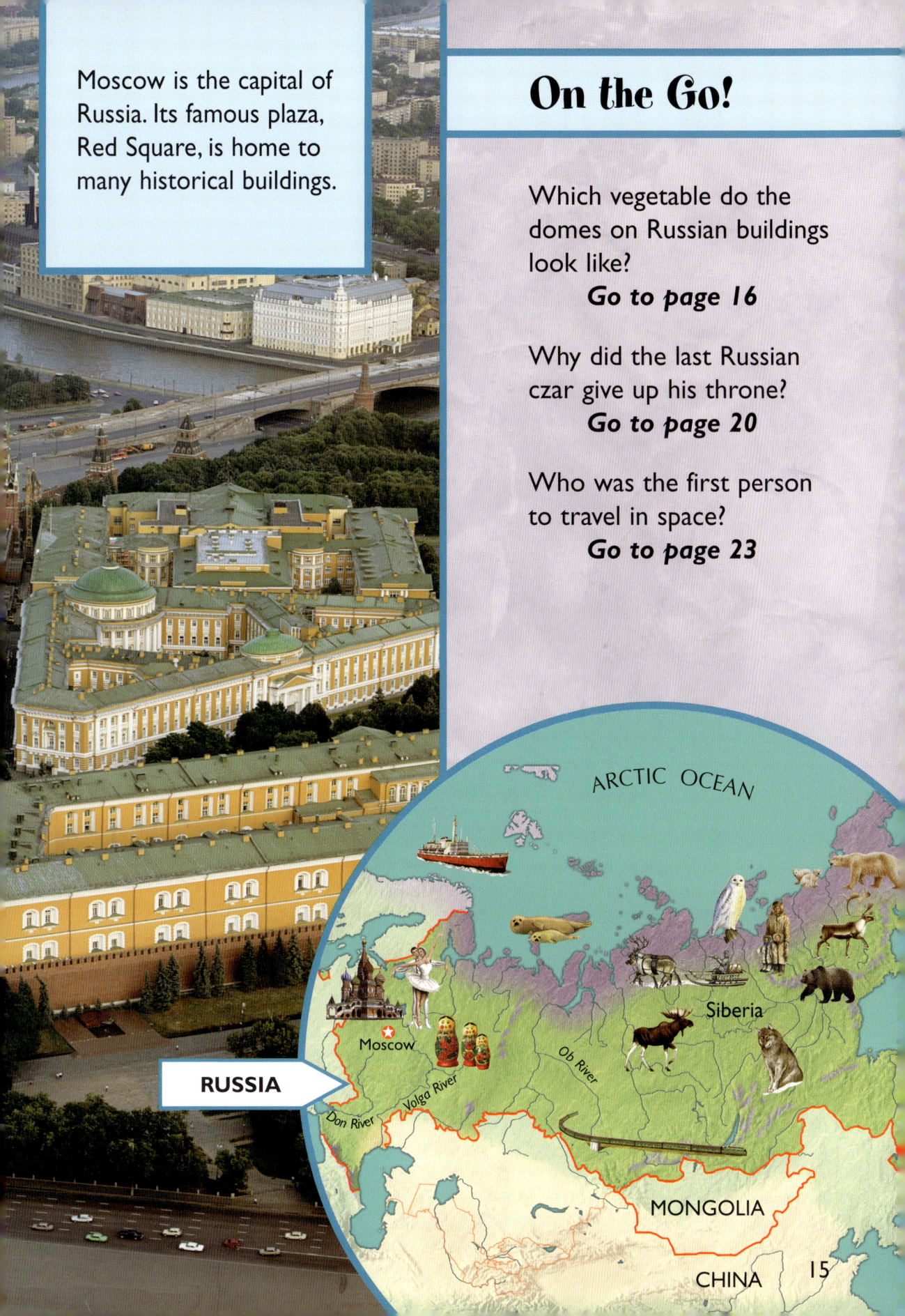

Moscow is the capital of Russia. Its famous plaza, Red Square, is home to many historical buildings.

On the Go!

Which vegetable do the domes on Russian buildings look like?
Go to page 16

Why did the last Russian czar give up his throne?
Go to page 20

Who was the first person to travel in space?
Go to page 23

ARCTIC OCEAN

Moscow

RUSSIA

Don River
Volga River
Ob River
Siberia

MONGOLIA

CHINA

Beautiful Buildings

One of the most beautiful buildings in Russia is the cathedral in Red Square. It has eight big domes. These domes have bright colors and a variety of patterns on them. Their onion shape lets snow slide off of them. Many Russian buildings and palaces have domes made from gold.

There are many beautiful palaces in Russia. They are richly decorated and often have gold statues and fountains outside. They were built to look like the great palaces of Europe.

cathedral   a large, important church

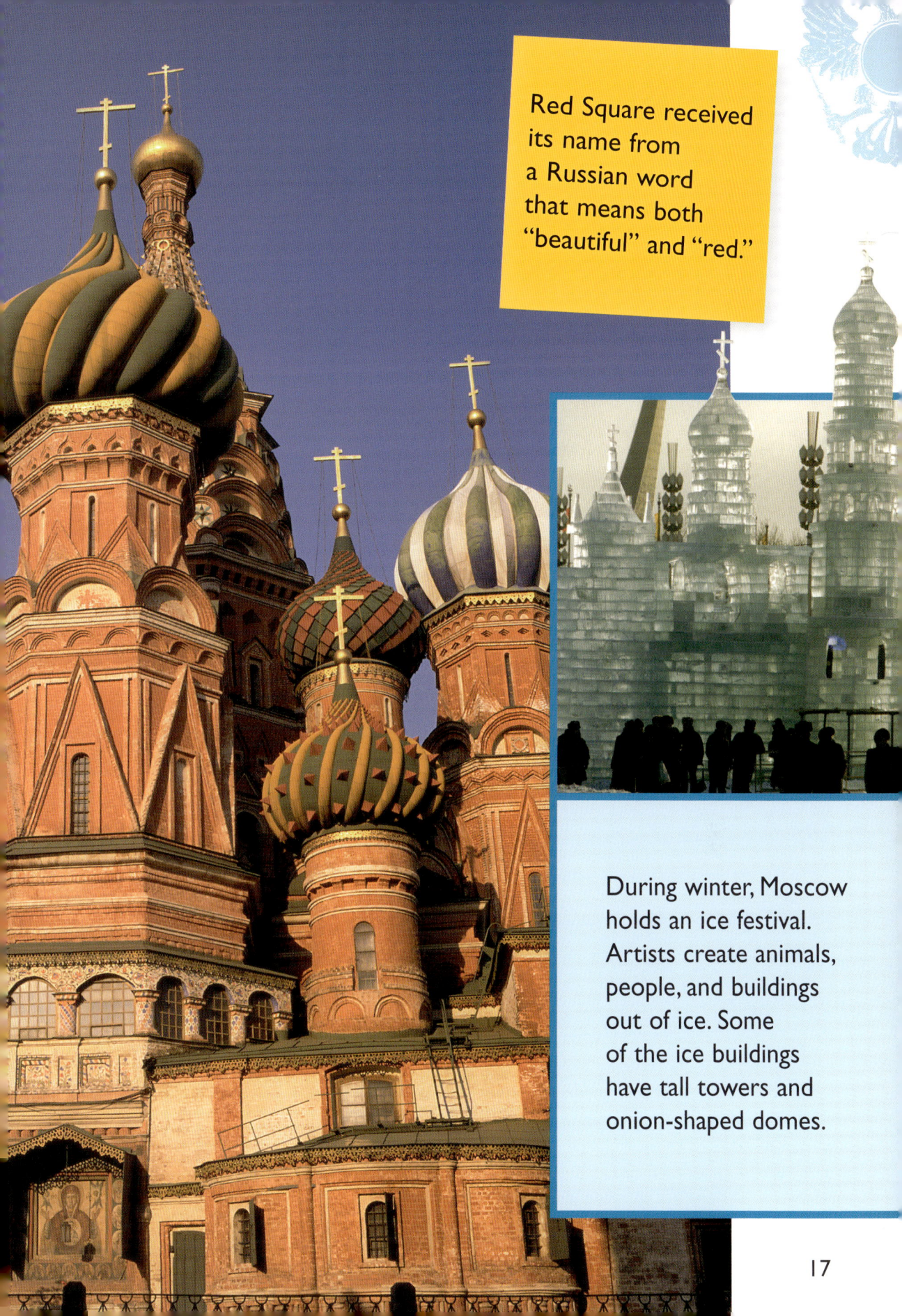

Red Square received its name from a Russian word that means both "beautiful" and "red."

During winter, Moscow holds an ice festival. Artists create animals, people, and buildings out of ice. Some of the ice buildings have tall towers and onion-shaped domes.

17

The Ballet

By the late 1800s, Russia was the ballet center of the world. World-famous ballets were performed throughout Russia. Russian composers wrote the music for many of the greatest ballets, such as *Sleeping Beauty* and *Swan Lake*.

Many of the greatest ballerinas and male dancers came from Russia, too. Anna Pavlova was famous during the early 1900s. Some of the best dancers toured or moved to other countries, introducing Russian ballet to the world.

Today, many Russian children still want to dance like the famous Anna Pavlova.

Anna Pavlova danced with the Imperial Ballet Company. She was the prima ballerina, or main female dancer.

The Royals of Russia

Russia's history goes back thousands of years. There were many great emperors and empresses. Peter I, also known as Peter the Great, built a new capital city and named it St. Petersburg. Catherine the Great ruled Russia for more than 30 years.

In 1917, royal rule in Russia came to a sudden end. Many Russian people fought against the royal family, so the czar, Nicholas II, was forced to give up his throne. His family, the Romanovs, was the last ruling family of Russia.

Russian protest, 1917

czar   a Russian emperor

Today, Russia's government has many political parties. Who governs your country?

Czar Nicholas II and his family

Russia on the Move

Russia led the world in space travel. In 1957, Russia launched *Sputnik*, the first human-made satellite to travel in space. A month later, the Russians sent a dog into space in *Sputnik 2*. Soon, the United States joined the space race.

Today, space travel is not a race. Countries that used to compete now work cooperatively in the exploration of space. In 1975, the crew of the American spaceship *Apollo* and the Soviet crew from *Soyuz* opened their airlocks, shook hands, and swapped gifts in space!

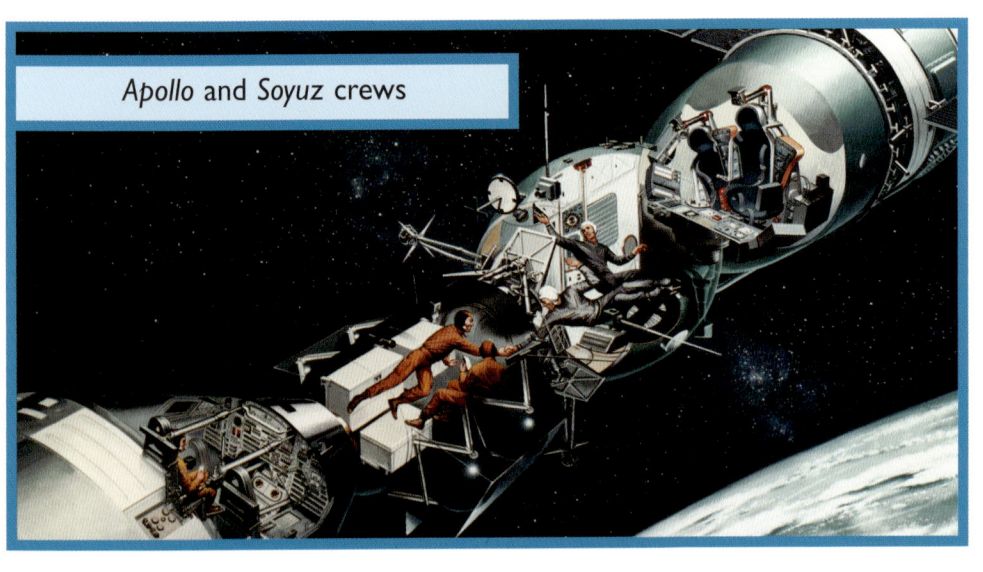

Apollo and *Soyuz* crews

On April 12, 1961, Russian cosmonaut Yuri Gagarin became the first person in space. His flight, aboard *Vostok 1*, orbited Earth in one hour and 48 minutes.

What other great events in space travel took place during the twentieth century?

What Do You Think?

1. What customs in Lena's daily life are the same as yours?

2. What things would be most difficult for you if you lived in Lena's town?

> Why would friendship be important in one of the coldest towns on Earth?

Index

animals	4, 6, 8, 11, 13, 22
ballet	18–19
buildings	15–17
climate	4–5, 7, 9, 11–14
royal family	20–21
schools	7
space travel	22–23